a writer's guide

to transitional words and expressions

Victor C. Pellegrino

Maui arThoughts Company
P.O. Box 967, Wailuku, HI, USA 96793-0967
Phone or Fax: 808-244-0156
Phone or Fax Orders Toll Free: 800-403-3472
E-mail: booksmaui@hawaii.rr.com
Website: www.booksmaui.com

International Standard Book Number: 0-945045-02-6
Library of Congress Card Number: 87-34726

Library of Congress Cataloging-in-Publication Data

Pellegrino, Victor C.

A Writer's Guide to Transitional Words and Expressions

1. English language — Rhetoric.
2. English language — Terms and phrases.
3. English language — Synonyms and antonyms — Glossaries, vocabularies, etc. I. Title.

PE1442.P45   1987   808'.042   87-34726

A mini-thesaurus consisting of more than 1,000 transitional words and expressions, divided and indexed into 15 categories; helps writers connect sentences and paragraphs; contains a supplemental section that lists over 500 substitutes for the word "said." This book is a companion text to *A Writer's Guide to Using Eight Methods of Transition*.

Cover and icons designed by Chris Magee

Published
by
Maui arThoughts Company
P.O. Box 967, Wailuku, HI, USA 96793-0967
Phone or Fax: 808-244-0156
Phone or Fax Orders Toll Free: 800-403-3472
E-mail: booksmaui@hawaii.rr.com
Website: www.booksmaui.com

DEDICATION

To my wife

Wallette Pualani Lyn-fah

To my children

Shelley Jeanne Laʻelaʻeokalā Lyn-oi
Angela Terese Mahinamālamalama Mei-lyn
Hōkūao Christopher Joseph Bailey Wu-wei

To my parents

Albert and Adeline Pellegrino

CONTENTS

INTRODUCTION

Almost anything you examine has some interrelationship or connection with something else. Buttons and buttonholes, for instance, join the two sides of a shirt; road signs allow you to drive from point A to point B without getting lost; train couplers link hundreds of freight cars. Sentences and paragraphs need to be connected, too. When you connect them, you provide a sense of movement that allows the reader to follow your ideas easily without becoming confused, disinterested, or frustrated. With clear, appropriate transitions, the reader will easily be able to distinguish your main idea from supporting ideas and understand how all of your ideas fit together.

Teachers and writers recognize eight separate methods of transition to connect ideas. These eight methods are: (1) using pronoun reference; (2) repeating key words; (3) using word substitution; (4) repeating key phrases; (5) using beginning-of-paragraph transition; (6) using end-of-paragraph transition; (7) embedding a transitional paragraph; and (8) using transitional words and expressions. The last of these eight methods, using transitional words and expressions, is possibly the most helpful, and it is the main focus of this book. To learn how to use all of the methods of transition, refer to the back pages of this book for information about how to obtain *A Writer's Guide to Using Eight Methods of Transition*.

Transitional words and expressions are called signal words. They are placed at key points in writing to lead the reader from one idea to the next. They help the reader move through sentences and paragraphs with an understanding of how the sentences and paragraphs relate to each other and to the written piece as a whole. At first, you might have the tendency to overuse transitional words and expressions. With practice, they will become a more natural part of your writing process.

A Writer's Guide to Transitional Words and Expressions is designed as a complementary text for *A Writer's Guide to Using Eight Methods of Transition*. Using both books regularly will help you learn how to create more effective and interesting writing. Your writing will be less redundant, more lively, and provide the connections readers need to follow your ideas—from point to point, from paragraph to paragraph, and from beginning to end.

When you write, keep this guide of over 1,000 transitional words and expressions nearby—at your desk, in the library, in the classroom, at the office, or next to your computer. Use both *A Writer's Guide to Transitional Words and Expressions* and *A Writer's Guide to Using Eight Methods of Transition* regularly to ensure that your writing is fluid, logical, and easy for your readers to follow. With practice, you will create smooth connections that will get results.

The last section of this book is a mini-thesaurus of 500 substitutes for the word *said*. It is especially helpful to keep this section open when you write dialogue. Whether writing short stories, children's books, novels, news stories, feature stories, poetry, biography, autobiography, reports, research papers, or letters, this list will help enliven your writing by adding greater variety and exactness—and by eliminating the overused word *said*.

A Writer's Guide
to
Transitional Words
and
Expressions

TO INDICATE TIME ORDER

past
in the past
in retrospect
before
earlier
heretofore
previously
preceding
former
formerly
prior to
yesterday
of late
recently
not long ago

present
at present
presently
currently
right away
now
by now
until
until now
today
immediately
simultaneously
at the same time
at this moment
concurrently
during
all the while

in the future
tomorrow
henceforth
hereafter

after
afterward
after a short time
after a while
after a long time
after a few days
soon after
soon afterward
thereafter
right after
not long after
later
later on
sequentially
following
following that

TO INDICATE HOW OR WHEN SOMETHING OCCURS IN TIME

suddenly
all at once
abruptly
in an instant
this instant
instantly
instantaneously
simultaneously
immediately
promptly
quickly
directly
soon, as soon as
just then
when

sometimes
some of the time
at times
in the meantime
occasionally
rarely, scarcely
seldom
uncommonly
infrequently
momentarily
temporarily
sporadically
intermittently
periodically
sequentially
cyclically
gradually
eventually
little by little
slowly
while, in a while
meanwhile

always
all of the time
every time
without exception
continually
at that time
at the same time
concurrently
repeatedly
often, oftentimes
frequently
generally, usually
as long as
at length
never, not at all

TO INDICATE SEQUENCE

first
at first
in the first place
once
once upon a time
begin
to begin with
at the beginning
at the onset
starting with
initially
commence
commencing with
embark
from this point
earlier

second
secondly
in the second place
the second stage
twice
next
the next day
the next time
the following week
then
after that
following that
immediately following
subsequently
on the next occasion
in turn
so far
later on

third
in the third place
last
last of all
at last
lastly
in the last place
the latter
at the end
in the end
ultimately
final
finally
the final point
to finish
to conclude
in conclusion
consequently

TO REPEAT

T
O

R
E
P
E
A
T

all in all
altogether
on the whole
in brief
in short
in effect
in fact
in particular
that is
simply stated
in simpler terms
to put it differently
in other words
again
once again
once more
again and again
over and over
to repeat
repeatedly
repetitively
a repetition of
repetitiously
to reword
as stated
as noted
in view of
in retrospect
that is to say
accordingly
to echo
to reecho
to reiterate
to restate
to retell
to recount
to review
to recapitulate
to retrace
to rephrase
to paraphrase
to refresh
to rethink
to reconsider
to reevaluate
to reexamine
to clarify
to explain
to outline
to summarize
in summary
a summation of

TO PROVIDE
AN EXAMPLE

for example   (e.g.,)
one example
as an example
to exemplify
for instance
in this instance
in this case
a case in point
to illustrate
as an illustration of
by way of illustration
consider as an illustration
to show
to demonstrate
to explain
to clarify
in order to clarify
to illuminate
to bring to light
an analogy
analogous to
suppose that
specifically
more specifically
in this instance
to be specific
to be exact
more exactly
in particular
more particularly
such as
namely
for one thing
that is   (i.e.,)
indeed
in fact
incidentally
in other words
to put it another way
thus
to cite a reference
one sample
a sampling
in the following manner
in the same manner
another way
at the same time

TO CONCEDE

of course
after all
granted
granted that
no doubt
at the same time
naturally
unfortunately
while it is true
although this may be true
though
although
even though
albeit
to acknowledge
to admit
admittedly
to admit the truth
to concede
to make a concession
to withdraw
to yield
to accede
to acquiesce
to capitulate
to surrender
to acknowledge defeat
to submit
to succumb
to give up
to compromise
to adjust
to settle
to confess
to accommodate
to conform
to reconcile
to agree
to consent
to concur
to comply with

TO CONCLUDE
OR SUMMARIZE

to conclude
in conclusion
to close
in closing
last
last of all
lastly
all in all
the final
finally
to finalize
to finish
to terminate
to end
to bring to an end
to complete
the completion of
to culminate
the culmination of
the outcome
the final outcome
thus
hence
therefore
the consequence
as a consequence of
consequently
as a result
the end result
in brief
in short
in other words
in sum
to sum up
in summary
to summarize
as a summation
to recapitulate
ultimately
accordingly

TO ADD A POINT

again
once again
and again
to repeat
repeatedly
also
too
as well as
besides
equally
equally important
first
first of all
in the first place
initially
primarily
for one thing
second
in the second place
secondarily
where . . . there
whether . . . or
third
last
last of all
final
finally
alternatively
further
furthermore
plus
in addition
in addition to
additionally
to add to that
not only . . . but also
another
more
moreover
once more
next
next to last
following
subsequently
likewise
similarly
in like manner
not unlike
above all
most of all
least of all
and
and then
or
either . . . or
nor
neither . . . nor
notwithstanding

however
yet
but
but . . . then
nevertheless
still
yet another
though
although
to continue
a continuation

TO COMPARE

as
as well as
like
look like
in like manner
likewise
liken (ed)
likeness
the next likeness
in much the same way
resemble
resembling
resemblance
a strong resemblance
affinity
correlate
parallel
parallel to
paralleling
homogeneous
consistent with
uniform
uniformly
same as
in the same way
in the same manner
just the same
to the same extent
at the same time
by the same token
synonymous with
identical
identically
of no difference
of little difference
equal
equally
equally important
equate
equivalent
relate to
akin
conform
harmonize
balance
coincide
match
matching
also
too
exactly
similarity
another similarity
similarly
similar to
in a similar fashion

analogous to
compare
comparatively
comparable
as compared with
a comparable aspect
in comparison
correspondingly
in relation to
relative to
relatively

TO CONTRAST

though
even though
although
although true
and yet
but
but at the same time
at the same time
despite
despite this fact
in spite of
even so
for all that
however
in contrast
in contrast to this
in sharp contrast
counter to
contrary to
on the contrary
to the contrary
contrarily
to contradict
contradictory
on one hand
on the other hand
in one way
in another way
although this may be true
nevertheless
nonetheless
notwithstanding
still
still another
yet
still yet
conversely
to differ
to differ from
to differentiate
different from
a clear difference
a distinct difference
a striking difference
distinct
a distinctive
another distinction
a strong distinction
the third distinction
unique
the next variation
otherwise
after all
instead
rather
unlike

an unlikeness
dissimilar to
a dissimilarity
unequal
unequally
unbalanced
disproportionately
unequivocally
larger
smaller
more
less
slower
faster
farther
further
opposite
opposing
to oppose
to counter
an opposing view
in opposition to
versus (v., vs.)
diametrically opposed
the reverse of
in reverse order
divergent
diverse
in conflict with
against
the antithesis of

TO INDICATE CAUSE AND EFFECT

accordingly
incidentally
by the way
owing to
effect
in effect
impact
due to
result
as a result
as a result of
resulted in
the end result
the end product
the by-product of
the outcome
the outgrowth
the aftermath
the ramifications of
as a consequence
consequently
consequentially
after
following that
eventually
further
furthermore
subsequently
it follows that
created
cause
caused by
because
because of
because of this
for this purpose
reason
for this reason
for these reasons
by reason of
in view of
hence
henceforth
otherwise
since
then
therefore
thereafter
thereupon
thus
to this end
with this object
so
in fact

of course
in short
little by little
gradually
on this account
on account of
made
produced
yielded
generated
induced
started
precipitated
initiated
launched

TO DIVIDE OR CLASSIFY

first
second
third
last
last of all
another type
another example
the next
one piece
a part
a second part
one of the
the second section
first step
second segment
third division
the last process
to classify
to group
another grouping
to split
to divide
to divide further
one genus
the second characteristic
another class
another category
in this category
subdivision
branch
unit
section
segment
segmentation
part
partition
element
the elements of
in the same group
in a different setting
with this arrangement
(un)common traits
the complete
completely
the entire
entirely
the whole
wholly
the single
the multiple
multilevel
multistage
multifaceted
to separate
separated from
to segregate
distinct from
to integrate
together with

TO INDICATE SPATIAL ARRANGEMENT

in	bordering
out	far
under	far away
over	far apart
above	far from
overhead	farther (est)
top	further (est)
at the top	furthermost
atop	remotest
on top of	in the distance
up, upper	beyond
upward	on one side
high (er/est)	on the other side
on	on the opposite side
off to the . . .	opposite to
below	facing
bottom	to the east, west . . .
near the bottom	straight ahead
on the bottom of	beside
at the base of	inside, interior
beneath	inward
down	inner (most)
downward	outside, exterior
low (er/est)	outward
behind	outer (most)
posterior	at the edge
to the back	alongside
toward the back	against the side
in the background	side by side
further back	on this side
in front	on all sides
anterior	underside
ahead of	surrounding
in the foreground	around
on the right	circling
to the right	encircling
right-hand	circular
on the left	perpendicular to
to the left	horizontally
left-hand	horizontal to
here	vertically
there	vertical to
thereabouts	paralleling
wherever	parallel to
elsewhere	level with
everywhere	at a tangent
anywhere	tangentially
near (est)	diagonally
nearby	between
close (est)	in between
close by	across
close to	among
close together	amid (st)
next to	in the middle
adjacent to	in the center
joining	midway
adjoining	at the midpoint
abutting	halfway
contiguous	in the corner
juxtaposed	at the corner
neighboring	at the end

TO EMPHASIZE OR INTENSIFY

above all
after all
indeed
in fact
as a matter of fact
primarily
chiefly
notably
actually
especially
secondarily
more important
more importantly
even more important
most important of all
most of all
increasingly important
equally
equally important
instead
moreover
furthermore
considerably more
significantly
the most significant
of great (er/est) concern
urgent
urgently
increasingly
more
more and more
incrementally
of major interest
notably
noteworthy
the chief characteristic
the most dramatic
the major point, reason
the main problem, issue
the most necessary
extremely
the utmost
exceedingly
overwhelmingly
repeatedly
to repeat
to recapitulate
to emphasize
more emphatically
of great (er) consequence
to accentuate
to underscore
to amplify
to enlarge
to highlight
to stress
strikingly

definitely
decidedly
by all means
unequivocally
you can be sure
undoubtedly
without doubt
without a doubt
doubtlessly
indubitably
certainly
absolutely
positively
surely
to be sure
of course
nonetheless
without fail
obviously
naturally
truly
verily
in truth
very likely
assuredly
to culminate
the culmination
the acme
the peak
the apex
the apogee
the crux
the climax of
the epitome
climactically
intensifying
to enlarge upon
to add to that
yes
without question
unquestionably
there is no question that
not the least of which

TO CONNECT CLAUSES

Use Coordinating Conjunctions

and
or
for
nor
but
yet
so

Use Correlative Conjunctions

both . . . and
either . . . or
neither . . . nor
not only . . . but also
whether . . . or
where . . . there

Use Subordinating Conjunctions

since	once
because	until
while	unless
though	before
although	after
as	that
as though	so that
even	in order that
even though	when
if	whenever
as if	than
even if	rather than

Use Conjunctive Adverbs

accordingly	thus
consequently	besides
as a result	also
certainly	anyway
finally	further
incidentally	furthermore
namely	in addition
for example	moreover
for instance	hence
similarly	henceforth
in the same way	however
undoubtedly	therefore
meanwhile	thereafter
nevertheless	subsequently
nonetheless	indeed
earlier	instead
now	likewise
then	otherwise
next	on the other hand
later	conversely
still	

Use Relative Pronouns

who	whoever
whom	whomever
which	whichever
that	whose

clause
clause

SUBSTITUTES FOR SAID

abided
accepted
accused
acknowledged
acquiesced
added
addressed
ad-libbed
admitted
admonished
advised
advocated
affirmed
agreed
aired
alleged
allowed
alluded
announced
answered
anticipated
appealed
approved
argued
articulated
asked
assented
asserted
assumed
assured
attested
averred
avowed

babbled
bantered
bargained
barked
bawled
bayed
began
begged
belittled
bellowed
bemoaned
beseeched
bickered
bid
bitched
blabbed
blabbered
blared
blasphemed
blasted
blurted (out)
boasted
boohooed
boomed
bragged
breathed
burst (out)

cackled
cajoled
calculated
called
carped
catechized
cautioned
chaffed
challenged
chanted
charged
chatted
chattered
cheered
chewed out
chided
chimed (in)
chirped
chortled
chuckled
cited
clacked
claimed
clamored
coaxed
commanded
commented
communicated
complained
complied
conceded
concluded
concurred
confessed
confided
confirmed
consented
contemplated
contended
contested
continued
contradicted
conversed
conveyed
cooed
corroborated
counseled
countered
crabbed
cracked
cried (out)
criticized
cross-examined
crowed
cursed

debated
decided
declaimed
declared
decreed

deemed
defended
deliberated
delivered
demanded
demurred
denied
denounced
deposed
derided
described
determined
dickered
dictated
differed
digressed
directed
disaffirmed
disagreed
disclosed
discussed
disputed
disrupted
divulged
doubted
drawled
driveled
droned

echoed
elaborated
elucidated
emitted
emphasized
encouraged
endorsed
entreated
entrusted
enumerated
enunciated
equivocated
estimated
eulogized
exclaimed
excogitated
explained
explicated
exploded
exposed
expounded
expressed
extemporized

faked
faltered
feared
figured
flirted
foretold
formulated
fumed

gabbed
gasped
giggled
gossiped
granted
greeted
grieved
grilled
grinned
griped
groaned
groped
groveled
growled
grumbled
grunted
guffawed
gulped
gurgled
gushed

haggled
hailed
harangued
harped (on)
hedged
held
hemmed and hawed
hesitated
hinted
hissed
hollered
hoped
howled
hummed

imagined
imitated
imparted
implied
implored
improvised
indicated
inferred
informed
injected
inquired
insinuated
insisted
instructed
insulted
interceded
interjected
interpolated
interposed
interpreted
interrogated
interrupted
intimated
introduced
invoked

itemized
iterated

jabbered
jawed
jeered
jested
jibed
joined in
joked
joshed
judged
justified

lamented
lashed out
laughed
let on
lied
lisped
listed

made known
maintained
mandated
marveled
mediated
mentioned
mimed
mimicked
minced
misconstrued
misquoted
misstated
moaned
mocked
moralized
mouthed
mumbled
murmured
mused
muttered

nagged
narrated
nasalized
needled
negotiated
noted
notified

objected
observed
opined
opposed
orated
ordered
overstated

panted
pantomimed

paraphrased
parleyed
parodied
parroted
pattered
peeped
persisted
persuaded
petitioned
phrased
piped in
pitched in
platitudinized
pleaded
pled
pledged
pointed out
pondered
pontificated
posited
postulated
praised
prated
prattled
prayed
preached
predicted
presented
pried
probed
proceeded
proclaimed
professed
prompted
pronounced
prophesied
proposed
propounded
protested
proved
publicized
pursued
put in

quarreled
queried
questioned
quibbled
quipped
quizzed
quoted

railed
rallied
rambled
ranted
rapped
rasped
rattled off (on)
raved
reaffirmed
reasoned
reassured
rebuffed
rebuked
rebutted
recanted
recapitulated
reciprocated
recited
reckoned
recommended
recounted
reechoed
reeled off
referred
reflected
refused
refuted
regretted
rehearsed
reiterated
rejoiced
rejoined
related
relented
remarked
reminded
remonstrated
renounced
repeated
repented
rephrased
replied
reported
reprimanded
reproached
requested
resounded
responded
restated
resumed
retold
retorted
retracted
returned
revealed
reviewed
rhapsodized
rhymed
ribbed
ridiculed
roared

roasted
ruled
rumored

sanctioned
sang
scoffed
scolded
scowled
screamed
screeched
scrutinized
sermonized
set forth
shouted
shrieked
sighed
signed
slandered
slobbered
slurred
smiled
snapped
snarled
sneered
snickered
sniggered
sniveled
snorted
snuffled
sobbed
solicited
soliloquized
somniloquized
spat out
specified
speculated
spewed
spieled (off)
spluttered
spoke (out)
spouted
sputtered
squawked
squeaked
squealed
squelched
stammered
stated
stipulated
stormed
stressed
stumbled
stuttered
submitted
suggested
summarized
summed up
summoned
supposed
swore

talked (on)
tattled
taunted
teased
tee-heed
testified
threatened
thundered
tittered
toasted
told
translated
transmitted
trumpeted
twitted
twittered

understated
upbraided
urged
uttered

vented
ventriloquized
ventured
verbalized
verified
vocalized
voiced
volunteered
vowed

wailed
warbled
warned
went on
wept
wheezed
whiffled
whimpered
whined
whispered
whistled
whooped
wished
wondered
wrangled

yackety-yakked
yakked
yapped
yawned
yawped
yelled
yelped
yipped
yoo-hooed

NOTES

NOTES

NOTES

NOTES

NOTES

BOOKS BY PELLEGRINO

A Writer's Guide to Transitional Words and Expressions
Pellegrino, © 1987, 1989, 1999; 8th printing, 2009
ISBN 0-945045-02-6, soft cover, $16.95

A Writer's Guide to Using Eight Methods of Transition
Pellegrino, © 1993; 2nd printing, © 2004 (Revised); 3rd printing, 2008
ISBN 0-945045-03-4, soft cover, $12.95

A Writer's Guide to Powerful Paragraphs
Pellegrino, © 2003, 2nd printing, 2009
ISBN 0-945045-05-0, soft cover, $24.95

A Writer's Guide to Perfect Punctuation
Pellegrino, © 2006, ISBN 0-945045-07-7, soft cover, $14.95

A Slip of Bamboo: A Collection of Haiku from Maui
Pellegrino, © 1996, ISBN 0-945045-04-2, soft cover, $9.95

Simply Bruschetta: Garlic Toast the Italian Way
Pellegrino, © 2001, ISBN 0-945045-06-9, hard cover, $18.95

Maui arThoughts: Expressions and Visions
Pellegrino, © 1988, ISBN 0-945045-01-8 (Out of Print)

You Can Write Workbook
Pellegrino, © 1983, ISBN 0-935848-28-2 (Out of Print)

You Can Write! Practical Writing Skills for Hawai'i
Pellegrino, © 1982, ISBN 0-935848-04-5 (Out of Print)

See ORDER FORM

Maui arThoughts Company

...the creative publisher with books that work...

P.O. Box 967, Wailuku, HI, USA 96793-0967
Phone/Fax Inquiries: 808-244-0156
Phone/Fax Orders Toll Free: 800-403-3472
E-mail: booksmaui@hawaii.rr.com   Website: www.booksmaui.com

ORDER FORM

●*Order by Mail... Phone... Fax... E-mail... or On-line*

MAIL ORDERS TO: Maui arThoughts Company
                   P.O. Box 967, Wailuku, HI, USA 96793-0967
PHONE or FAX FOR INFORMATION/INQUIRIES: 808-244-0156
PHONE or FAX ORDERS TOLL FREE: 800-403-3472
E-MAIL ORDERS TO: booksmaui@hawaii.rr.com
WEBSITE: www.booksmaui.com

●PLEASE SEND ME (Indicate Number of Copies in Boxes)

☐	*A Writer's Guide to Powerful Paragraphs* @ \$24.95 per copy, ISBN 0-945045-05-0	\$ +
☐	*A Writer's Guide to Transitional Words & Expressions* @ \$16.95 per copy, ISBN 0-945045-02-6	\$ +
☐	*A Writer's Guide to Using Eight Methods of Transition* @ \$12.95 per copy, ISBN 0-945045-03-4	\$ +
☐	*A Writer's Guide to Perfect Punctuation* @ \$14.95 per copy, ISBN 0-945045-07-7	\$ +
	SUBTOTAL	\$

●DISCOUNTS (Include Purchase Order)

Retail Bookstores, less 40%	\$ –
College/University Bookstores, less 20%	\$ –
Schools & Libraries, less 10%	\$ –

●TAXES

Hawai'i Residents (Include .04166 Sales Tax)	\$ +
Hawai'i Bkstrs., Schools & Libraries (Include .005 Whsl. Tax)	\$ +

●SHIPPING & HANDLING (2 Choices)

1) For 1 copy: \$5.75 USPS Priority Mail. Add \$.50 for each   \$ +
     additional book up to 10 copies

2) For more than 10 books, we will bill you for S & H.
     Please check your selection below:
     ☐USPS Priority Mail
     ☐UPS 2nd Day Air
     ☐UPS Ground

TOTAL AMOUNT DUE	\$

●PAYMENT

Choose to pay now or later. We will bill you for S & H as needed.
☐Check/Money Order (make payable to Maui arThoughts Company)
☐Purchase Order Number (Attach P.O. to Order Form)
☐Bill Me Later

●BILL TO ADDRESS   ●SHIP TO ADDRESS

Name _____   Name _____

Address_____   Address_____

City _____ State ___ Zip_____   City _____ State ___ Zip_____

●**NOTE**   All prices are subject to change without notice.

ABOUT THE AUTHOR

Victor C. Pellegrino, Professor Emeritus, taught writing and literature at Maui Community College for twenty-eight years, and served eight years as chairperson of the Language Arts Division. He has also taught upper division classes in advanced writing and American literature for the University of Hawai'i on Maui.

Recognized as a statewide leader in the field of writing, Pellegrino was the first recipient of the Excellence in English Teaching Award presented by the Hawai'i affiliate of the National Council of Teachers of English. He also received the Excellence in Teaching English Award from the Hawai'i Branch of the English-Speaking Union of the United States. Pellegrino has served on the editorial board of *Makali'i, The Journal of the University of Hawai'i Community Colleges*, and has edited for publication many manuscripts.

During his teaching career, Pellegrino developed a unique interdisciplinary Eastern world literature course emphasizing the writings of India, China, and Japan. This course complemented Pellegrino's Western world literature course emphasizing Europe, Africa, and Russia. He also taught British and American literature.

Pellegrino's books have guided writers for two decades. In 1984, he wrote two books designed for use in Hawai'i schools, *You Can Write! Practical Writing Skills for Hawai'i* and *You Can Write Workbook* (both out-of-print). *A Writer's Guide to Transitional Words and Expressions* was first published in 1987 (8th printing, 2009). *A Writer's Guide to Using Eight Methods of Transition*, published in 1993 (3rd printing, 2008), serves as a complementary text to his popular transitional words book. *A Writer's Guide to Powerful Paragraphs*, his third title in the writer's guide series, was published in 2003 (2nd printing, 2009), and focuses on thirty different ways to organize and write effective paragraphs. In 2006, he added a fourth title to his writing series, *A Writer's Guide to Perfect Punctuation*.

Pellegrino's writings are not limited to the world of English. *Maui Art Thoughts: Expressions and Visions* (out-of-print) focuses on his philosophical aphorisms. *A Slip of Bamboo: A Collection of Haiku from Maui* contains selections from the hundreds of haiku he has been writing since 1973. In 2001, he published an Italian cookbook, *Simply Bruschetta: Garlic Toast the Italian Way*. He completed his first family history, *The Falcone Family (La Famiglia Falcone)* in 2007. He is currently working on a novel, a children's allegory, a vegetable-based Italian cookbook, as well as his second family history, The Pellegrino Family (La Famiglia Pellegrino).

In addition to his own writing, Pellegrino has edited and assisted in the publication of numerous books for authors from Hawai'i and the Mainland as well as conducted self-publishing seminars for Maui Community College's Department of Continuing Education and Hawai'i Writer's Conference. As a cookbook author, Pellegrino has appeared on television shows, in Hawai'i and on the Mainland. He has held numerous food demonstrations, taught many cooking classes, served as guest chef, and conducted cookbook writing workshops.

Pellegrino received B.S. and M.S. degrees from the SUNY, Buffalo. He has studied and traveled extensively in Japan and China. In 1984, he was a Fulbright Scholar in India. He is married to Wallette Garcia. They have three children, Shelley, Angela, and Hōkūao, and two grandchildren, Jonathan and Ryan.